I0056819

Options Trading

*How to Make Money in Less
Than 7 Days*

Table of Contents

© Copyright 2018 by Victor Lucas - All rights reserved.

The transmission, duplication or reproduction of any of the following work, including specific information will be considered an illegal act irrespective of if it is done electronically or in print. This extends to creating a secondary or tertiary copy of the work or a recorded copy and is only allowed with an express written consent from the Publisher. All additional right reserved.

The information in the following pages is broadly considered to be a truthful and accurate account of facts and as such any inattention, use or misuse of the information in question by the reader will render any resulting actions solely under their purview. There are no scenarios in which the publisher or the original author of this work can be in any fashion deemed liable for any hardship or damages that may befall them after undertaking information described herein. The author does not take any responsibility for inaccuracies, omissions, or errors which may be found therein.

Additionally, the information in the following pages is intended only for informational purposes and should thus be thought of as universal. As befitting its nature, it is presented without assurance regarding its prolonged validity or interim quality. The author of this work is not responsible for any loss, damage, or inconvenience caused as a result of reliance on information as published on, or linked to, this book.

The author of this book has taken careful measures to share vital information about the subject. May its readers acquire the right knowledge, wisdom, inspiration, and succeed.

Introduction

Congratulations on downloading this book and thank you for doing so.

The following chapters will teach you the ins and outs of options trading:

Chapter 1 talks about the basics so that you will have a good foundation and understanding of what options trading is really all about.

Chapter 2 discusses the risks and benefits of options trading.

Chapter 3 teaches powerful and effective strategies that you can use to increase your chances of making the right trading decisions.

Chapter 4 reveals the important keys to success to help make you a better options trader.

Chapter 5 lays down the common mistakes that you should avoid.

Chapter 6 discusses the successful trader's mindset. It is the right mindset if you want to make continuous profits with options trading.

May this book be your guide to success, happiness, and financial freedom

There are plenty of books on this subject on the market, thanks again for choosing this one! Every effort was made to ensure it is full of as much useful information as possible. Please enjoy!

Chapter 1: Options Trading 101

What is options trading?

Options trading is also called *binary options*. It is like trading stocks and forex. However, you do not have to purchase any assets. Instead, you simply have to speculate if the price of a particular asset will increase or decrease at expiry date. Many traders get attracted to options trading due to its simplicity. It is also worth noting that this kind of trading has a fixed risk as well as a fixed payout.

Options trading vs. gambling

There are people who confuse options trading with gambling. In fact, in some jurisdictions, trading options is already considered as gambling. Just like a game of roulette where you can wager if the ball will land on red or black, in options trading, you simply have to speculate if the price of an underlying asset will rise or fall at a specified time. Also, just like many gambling games, there is a fixed payout if you are able to predict the outcome correctly.

Does this mean that options trading is gambling? Well, it depends on how you approach it. If you trade options by relying on mere guesswork, then you can consider that to be gambling. But if every "wager" that you make is backed up with a thorough research and a good understanding of the asset concerned, and if you consider every decision as an investment decision, then you are trading/investing and not just gambling. Take note that this does not necessarily mean that gambling is completely bad, especially once you witness how the casino sharks dominate a table. However, it is not advisable to approach options trading as a mere gamble, because doing so can significantly increase the chances of losing all your investment. Now, whether you view options trading as gambling or not is a free choice that you can make. The important thing here is the profit that you have earned if any.

Options trading vs. forex and stock trading

When you trade options, you do not have to buy currencies or stocks. You do not get to own any assets. Instead, you merely speculate if the price of a particular asset will rise or fall at expiry date. Another distinct difference is that when you trade options, there is a fixed payout. You will know how much you will earn if you make the right decisions. When you trade forex or stocks, there is no fixed profit potential. You cannot tell the exact profit that you can earn. Also, when you trade currencies or stocks, you will normally have to wait for long weeks and months just to earn a significant amount of profit. When you trade options, you can earn even as high as 1,000% of your investment quickly, even in as fast as a few minutes. Of course, this is not that easy to do, but it is possible as long as you can speculate the price movements correctly. When you trade options, there are fewer fees for you to worry about. There is no need for you to be concerned of any surcharges, volume restrictions, and others. Last but not least, it is much easier to learn trading options than forex or stock trading.

Is it for you?

So, is options trading for you? It is true that almost anyone can start trading options right away, but not everyone can achieve success with options trading. To increase your chances of making continuous profits, you should put in enough time and efforts. If you are not willing to do serious research and analysis, then perhaps options trading is not for you. It is not uncommon for professional options traders spend long hours in research and analysis. You simply cannot rely on mere guesswork. You have to study the market and the assets that you are dealing with. Whether options trading is for you or not is something that only you can decide. The good news is that it is something that you can learn. Even if you think that you do not have what it takes to be a successful options trader at the present time, you can still make adjustments and learn to be a great options trader.

Assets

Options trading is about speculating the price movement of a particular asset. You should predict if its price will rise higher or fall lower than its current price at expiry date. What are assets? Assets are usually defined as "financial instruments that have value." When you trade options, there are different assets that you can work on, such as stocks, commodities, and currency pairs, among others.

Call/Put

When you trade options, you just have to choose between two decisions: call or put. You should choose to *call* if you speculate that the price of the asset will be higher than its current price at expiry time, and you should choose the *put* option if you think that the value of an asset will be lower than its current price at expiry time.

Take note that some trading platforms use other terms for these. You may encounter terms like up and down, above and below, high and low, rise and fall, and others. However, they all refer to the same choices that you have when you trade options: call vs. put.

Strike price

For a Call option, the strike price represents the price at which the asset can be bought at a specified time. For a Put option, the strike price signifies the price at which an underlying asset may be sold.

Expiry date

The expiry date simply refers to the end of a trading period. This is the time when you will know if you have made the right (or wrong) trading decision. When you trade options, you can choose the time frame just how long you want it to last. You can choose an expiry date that is a long way from now, but you can also choose a trading period that is as fast as a few minutes or even as quick as 60 seconds. In choosing the right expiry date for you, you should consider the kind of strategy that you are using. For example, technical analysis is an excellent strategy for trades that have a short timeframe. Do not worry; we will tackle this strategy later in the book. For now, just read and focus on learning the basics.

Long-term option vs. Speed option

As the name implies, a long-term option is one that lasts for a long period of time. However, the word "long" is relative. In options trading, long-term options are options are last for at least 24 hours or longer. Speed option is the kind of option that has a shorter period. It can take just a few hours, but it can also be as fast as a minute or so. This is as close as you can get to casino gambling.

In-the-money vs. Out-the-money

In-the-money refers to a winning trade. Hence, it means profit. It signifies that you have made the right decision and won a trade. On the contrary, out-the-money means that you just lost a trade.

Bear market vs. Bull market

These two terms describe the status of the market. When you say that it is a bear market, it means that the prices of assets are falling or are just about to decrease. When you say that the market is a bull market, it means that the prices of certain assets are increasing or are about to increase. Now, unlike trade stocks or currencies, you can still earn money from options trading even in the case of a bear market. This is because your profits do not rely on the prices of assets, but if you are able to predict or speculate their price movements. This is one of the best reasons to trade options. You can still make a substantial amount of profits regardless of the situation of assets in the market.

What to look for in an options trading broker

Before you can start trading options, you first need to open an account with a broker. When you make a search online, you will find a long list of brokers that seem to offer the same service. So, how do you know which one will best suit your needs? Here are the set standards to look for:

- Trading platform

It should be noted that it is your broker that will provide you with the platform that you can use for options trading. As a rule, it should make the experience of trading more convenient and fun for you. The platform should be easy to use. Although the design of the platform is not considered very important by some traders, it is still a good idea to pick a platform that is professionally designed as it can help to put you in the right mood for trading. The platform should also provide you with free tools, such as graphs, to help you come up with the best trading decision.

- Customer support

It is extremely important that you work with a broker that has an active and reliable customer support team. The support team can be helpful, especially if you encounter technical problems or if you simply have any inquiry regarding the trading platform. A broker will give you some ways to reach the support team. Normally, the customer support can be contacted via email, or via on-page chat. There might also be a number that you can call. Make sure that you take note of the way/ways that your broker provides to contact the support team.

- Mobile feature

These days, it is much easier to access the Internet on your mobile device, and brokers are well aware of this. This is why most, if not all, of the top brokers out there offer a mobile feature of the trading platform. This will allow you to engage in options trading at any time by simply using your mobile phone. Normally, you will not be able to use all the features of the trading platform if you use the mobile feature, but it should allow you to use the important parts of the platform, such as being able to place your trade, make deposits and a withdrawals, and others.

- Demo account

Your broker should provide you with a demo account. The demo account will allow you to make trades in a real options trading environment without risking anything. It is also a good tool to use when testing out your strategy. If you are just starting out, then you are encouraged to practice with the demo account until you become familiar with the actual practice of options trading.

- Positive reviews

Before you make a deposit into your trading account, you should first check the reviews given to your broker. This is easy to do: Simply use your favorite browser, type the name of the broker, add the word "reviews," and then press the *enter* key. The search engine results page (SERP) will then show you relevant pages. Make sure that your broker has positive reviews. Also, pay attention to the dates when the reviews were made. You want to read the latest reviews. It is okay if a broker has some negative reviews as long as the positive reviews outweigh the negative. It is important that you only work with a reliable broker. Unfortunately, there are many scammers online who only want to rip you off of your money. By checking the latest reviews, you can lower the chances of having to deal with an unreliable broker.

- Availability of assets

It is good if your broker has a wide selection of assets. Although this is not required as you can always make a profit despite the status of the market. In options trading, the only important thing is to make the right speculations. Even if the price of an asset drops, you can still make a nice profit. This is one of the reasons why so many people these days want to learn about options trading. There is always the opportunity to make a high profit regardless of the current market situation.

- Payout

Different brokers may offer different payouts. Choose a broker that offers a high payout. Ideally, your broker should offer a payout of at least 85%. Some brokers even give a payout as high as 90% or even 95%. Just be sure to work with a trustworthy broker.

- Banking options

Be sure to check the banking options provided by your broker. It is not uncommon for brokers provide more ways to make a deposit, but only limited methods for making a withdrawal. Make sure that the options offered by your broker are available for you for making a deposit and withdrawal. You should also check the requirements that your broker might impose when requesting for a withdrawal. It is common for brokers to ask for copies of certain documents, such as a valid ID and a proof of billing before they even start to process a withdrawal request. Make sure that you have such documents in your possession and that they have not yet expired. If you have more concerns about this matter, kindly contact the customer support team. you want to avoid the situation where you have lots of funds and profits in your account but have no way of withdrawing them.

- Security

Your broker should offer powerful security. Ideally, your broker's site should be encrypted especially every time that you need to input sensitive information like your password. There are many hackers online, so be sure that you also focus on the security of your account. If your broker offers additional security features like a two-factor authenticator where you will have to input a code after your password to access your account, then be sure to make use of them also. Although this might seem a hassle for a beginner, it also helps to ensure the security of your trading account. Also, you will probably have to leave your money in your account, so you really have to use a secure site so that you would not have to worry about losing your funds. Make security a priority. Unfortunately, some traders only realize the importance of having tight security after they have already lost their funds. By then, it is already too late.

Remember that when it comes to the money or funds that you keep online, having a strong security should be a primary priority.

Chapter 2: Risks and Benefits

Risks

- Market risk

Whether you make a profit or not will depend on the price movement of the asset involved, and this price movement depends on how the market behaves. It is difficult to tell the direction that the market will take. This simply depends on so many factors that are outside of your control. Hence, no matter how much research you do, never forget this element of market risk.

- Lack of ownership

When you trade binary options, you do not get to own the stock or commodity that is being traded. You are merely speculating its price movement, whether it is going to rise or fall at expiry time. You do not exercise any form of ownership.

- High risk

Options trading is a high-risk investment. Although you can earn even as high as 90% or even higher in a single trade, there is a risk of losing all of your invested funds in a trade if you make the wrong decision. This means that if, for example, you wager $200, and you lose the trade, then you will lose the whole $200 instantly. This is unlike trading forex or stocks where you still retain ownership over what is left and be able to sell them to at least recover some of your losses. But, do not let this discouraged you as the profit potential in options trading is also very high. As the saying goes, "high risk, high return."

- Not liquid

Options do not have any liquidity. If you enter into a trade, you will have to wait for the trading period to end. In the meantime, you simply have to hope for the best. There are traders who will allow you to cancel a trade, but this is normally exercised only in a short timeframe and can even come with a fee. This is usually used only when you enter a trade by mistake. However, you should also understand that liquidity should not be much of an issue when you trade options since you can choose to trade within a short timeframe only, even as fast as 1 minute.

- Limited potential profit

When you trade options, there is already a predetermined payout even before you enter into a trade. Therefore, you will already know just how much you can earn. Of course, in case you make the wrong trading decision, you will lose all the funds that you invested in a trade. This is unlike investing in stocks or currencies where there is no particular ceiling as to how much you can earn. However, it is also noteworthy that when you invest in stocks, a profit of 25% in a year is already considered high. Since currencies are already well established and are strictly regulated, their prices do not fluctuate significantly. Now, compare this with the around 90% profit potential when you trade options which you can earn in just a few minutes.

- High probability of losing

It is true that many people who invest in options trading lose their money. Although you may encounter stories of people who triple or even multiply their money by more than five times in a few minutes, there are many other stories where they lose all their funds in one trading day. Just as you options trading can make you money quickly, it can also cause you to lose all your funds quickly. This is why you need to understand it and develop an effective strategy.

Benefits

- High return

If you think that a 30% profit is already considered high, wait until you see how much you can earn when you trade options. With options trading, you can earn as high as around 90% in a single trade, which can be as fast as one minute. There are, of course, other time frames that you can use.

- Simple

Options trading is not a complicated process. It is just like predicting the outcome of a coin flip. In this case. You simply have to decide if it is going to be a call or a put. Indeed, you can easily learn how to trade options in just a few minutes.

- A wide range of assets

With binary options, you will have a lot of choices as to where to put an investment. After all, you would not purchase any stock or asset. In fact, some brokers will allow you to trade with a minimum amount of $1. If you use bitcoins, you can even find brokers that will allow you to trade binary options, even with less than a dollar per trade.

- Limited risk

You do not have to worry about risking more than you can afford to lose. There are no surcharges or any other hidden charges for you to worry about. The extent of your risk is limited to the amount of your wager.

- Gambling factor

Gambling is fun. This is why many people get addicted to it. When you deal with options trading there is this gambling factor that you can enjoy. However, it is noteworthy that you should not allow this gambling impulse to take control of your decisions. If you want to have consistent success with trading binary options, you should take the time and efforts to study the different assets, develop a strategy, and come up with the right trading decisions.

- Quick

When you trade options, there are different timelines that you can choose from. A trade can last for days and weeks, but you can also choose a timeline that is as fast as an hour, five minutes, or even just one minute. Some brokers even offer a timeframe of less than one minute. Hence, if you are interested in making quick trades, then you should definitely look into options trading.

Now that you know the benefits and risks associated with options trading, are you still willing to pursue it? If you take a closer look, you will realize that the benefits completely outweigh the risks involved. After all, in any investment or trade, there are always risks involved. It will just depend on how much risk you are willing to handle. If you are still deciding to pursue options trading, then it is time for you to learn effective strategies that can help pave your way to success.

Chapter 3: Powerful Strategies

When you trade options, you need to apply the right strategies to increase your chances of making the right trading decisions. It is not a good idea to just gamble and rely solely on luck. If you want to have continuous success trading binary options, then you must approach it the right way: by using powerful and effective strategies.

> ➢ Fundamental analysis

Fundamental analysis is considered to be the *lifeblood of investment*. It is probably one of the most important strategies that you should use. In fact, expert traders advise that if you are serious about trading options, then you should definitely make use of fundamental analysis.

As the name implies, this strategy deals with the fundamentals or the basics. This is important since it deals with the foundation of the asset involved. Take note, however, that fundamental analysis is not limited to just the asset itself, but also takes into consideration other factors, such as the economy, current market trend, competition, and technological developments, among others. The idea behind this strategy is that by studying and analyzing the fundamentals, you will be more able to come up with the right trading decision. For example, if there is a news piece that states that the employment rate in the U.S. has significantly increased, there is a good chance that the price of USD will increase. This will allow you to make the right options trading decision since you now have an idea of the direction that the USD will take.

Fundamental analysis is not just about the economy. One of the major forces that drive the economy is business. Therefore, you need to take a closer look and study various businesses, as well as how they affect one another. You have to analyze their financial statements, their competitors, and their performance in the market, among others. It is also noteworthy that fundamental analysis can be applied together with another strategy.

Indeed, this approach is probably one that demands the most time and efforts, but it is very much worth it. In fact, it would be rare to find a successful and professional options trader who does not use fundamental analysis on a regular basis. Keep in mind that the more that you understand the basics, the more that you can come up with the right trading decision.

➤ Technical analysis

This strategy makes use of graphs and charts, so if you are more of a visual person, then you will most likely enjoy using this strategy. With technical analysis, you will analyze the performance of an underlying asset to predict its future movement. If you are not fond of analyzing hard facts and numbers, then this strategy is the way to go. The charts and graphs will show you the price movements of the asset concerned over a period of time. The idea behind this approach is that the different factors that can affect an asset has had their final effect on the price. Therefore, by simply dealing directly with the price movements, you also get to deal with all these factors. This makes the work much simpler and more direct. After all, whether you make a profit or not will depend on how the price of an asset moves.

When you use technical analysis, the key is to learn to identify and take advantage of patterns.

However, the problem is that patterns come and go. Therefore, just because you have studied a particular graph for an hour does not always mean that there is a pattern for you to see. A common mistake is to force to see a pattern even when it does not really exist. Remember to never create a pattern when it is not there. You need to keep an open and unbiased mind when you examine any graph or chart. Again, it is your broker that should provide you with helpful tools like graphs/charts.

Do patterns really exist? The answer here is *yes*. In fact, even a random generator creates patterns every now and then. Once you spot a pattern, then you will know how an asset will move, and you can use that to your advantage. Just remember to be careful with identifying a pattern since patterns come and go.

Just like fundamental analysis, you can safely apply technical analysis to another strategy. In fact, many expert traders combine fundamental analysis and technical analysis.

> Go with the flow

This is a very common strategy used even by those who have not read anything about options trading. So, be careful when you use this strategy. As the name already implies, it means that you simply have to follow the flow or trends. This is a good strategy for a speed option so that you would not miss the trend. However, do not just follow any increase or decrease in value of an underlying asset. Instead, analyze the graph and try to look for a pattern.

➢ Double down

The double down strategy is based on the martingale strategy as used in casino gambling. It is a betting strategy that will allow you to recover all your losses and always make a profit each time you make the right decision. As the name suggests, you simply have to double the amount that you wager every time you encounter a loss. Once you make a winning trade, then you should go back to your base amount (the original amount that you wager). Here is an example: Let us say that you start with $5. If you lose the trade, then your next wager should be $10. Again, if it loses, then wager $20, and so on and so forth. Simply put, just double the wager every time you encounter a loss. If you make the right speculation, then you will be able to recover all of your losses plus a profit. However, take note that options trading does not give back 100%, so you might want to compute the exact amount that you will earn. Be careful; although this may seem like a practical strategy to use, it is also considered highly aggressive. Therefore, use this strategy sparingly.

➤ Conservative betting

This is an excellent betting strategy to use if you are just starting out. But, it is also a good strategy for advanced traders. The key here is to be as conservative as possible. You can do this by using flat betting. It is also advised that you only use a maximum of 2%-3% of your total funds per trade. When you use this approach, you should focus on increasing your success rate. Since you will be using flat betting, you will most likely end up in positive profit provided you maintain a high success rate. To have a high success rate, be sure that every trade that you make is backed up by a solid research.

➤ Mixed

There are also those who suggest that you should not stick to using the same strategy all the time. After all, the market itself does not observe the same behavior all the time. It always changes. The prices of certain assets rise as others fall, and this can continue, but the opposite can also happen. If you use this approach, you can use one strategy for your first trade, and then a different strategy on your next trade and so on. Obviously, this requires more efforts as you will have to learn and practice the different strategies.

> Asset mastery

The aim of this strategy is to gain mastery over a particular asset. Pick an asset that you want to invest in. Now, make it a priority to read and learn something about that asset every day. After some time, you will have a good understanding of that asset. Learn as much as you can about it. Be sure to spare some time every day to understand the said asset. You will soon notice that you are more able to predict its price movement easily. Once you reach this level, then that is the time for you to use real money and place a wager. Once you gain mastery over a particular asset, then you can jump to another asset. However, remember not to forget about the previous asset/assets that you have mastered.

There is really no such thing as "mastery" of an asset; however, you will know if you are ready to make a real-money trade if you are confident of your understanding of a particular asset. The key to this strategy is gaining more understanding about an asset so that you will be able to speculate its price movement more effectively.

> Co-integration trading strategy

This strategy relies on the strong correlation between two underlying assets. This usually takes place when two assets belong to the same industry or share the same market.

Due to the high correlation, you will notice that their prices are almost always close to each other. In case there happens to be a significant gap between the prices of the two assets, which usually occurs when one of them has become weak, such gap is only temporary. Due to their high correlation, the prices will adjust again be somewhat close. If you ever notice this, then you are already one step ahead. The only thing left for you to find out now is either to place a *call* on the asset whose price has dropped or a *put* on the asset with a higher price.

➢ Corrective

You can use this strategy when you see a sudden surge in price, either a dramatic increase or decrease. Take note that such price spike is only brief and temporary. Soon, the price will balance by returning to its value just before the spike, or at least somewhere close to it. When you see this kind of trend, then you are one step ahead, and you can better make the right trading decision.

> ➤ Make your own

You should realize that you are dealing with a continuously moving and evolving market. So, feel free to come up with your own strategy. You can either develop the strategies that you already know or create something that is totally new. The important thing is that it should work and help rake in positive profits. When you work as a serious trader, it is common to always be working on a strategy. You can expect to do countless of trial and error just to learn and develop an effective strategy. This is simply a normal part of the life of an options trader.

Chapter 4: Keys to Success

✓ Do not chase after your losses

This is a common advice that is given to gamblers, but it also applies when you engage in binary options. "Do not chase after your losses." A quite surprising fact is that those who are well aware of this teaching still fall into this trap. So, how does this work? Chasing after your losses normally happen after you experience a bad loss. The tendency is that you will feel that you have to recover what you have lost and perhaps even profit even by a little. After all, you have already spent time and efforts, so you should at least gain something. However, the problem here is that it tends to change your strategy into an aggressive one. This is because when you chase after your losses, you will have to wager a higher amount since you will take your previous loss into consideration. You will only earn a fixed percentage, so if you want to gain a bigger profit, which would be enough to cover your past loss/losses, then you will have to invest a bigger amount in the next trade. The problem is that there is no amount of research that can guarantee a favorable outcome of a trade. Doing your research and applying the strategies can only increase your chances of making the right trading decision, but they could not guarantee the return of positive profits. So, if you lose your trade again, then just imagine how many losses you will suffer. You should also keep in mind that it is not considered uncommon to experience four, five, or even higher, losing trades in a row, especially if you do not take the time to do all the necessary research and analysis.

This does not mean that chasing after your losses will always end up in a bad way. If you get lucky, you might be able to recover all of your losses and even earn a nice profit. However, the probability of this from happening is quite low. In fact, if you continue to chase after your losses, there is more than a 90% chance that you will end up losing all your funds in the long run due to the highly aggressive approach that it involves. Instead of chasing after your losses, the better advice is to focus on chasing after more profits. Do not allow your losing trades to discourage you. After all, even advanced traders still experience some losing trades every now and then. The important thing is to end up in a positive profit once you add up everything together.

✓ The importance of keeping a journal

Although not considered a requirement, it can still be helpful to write a trading journal. In fact, many expert traders strongly recommend the use of a journal. A trading journal will allow you to view yourself from a new and unbiased perspective. This way, you can more easily identify your strengths and weaknesses. Do not worry; you do not have to be a professional writer to write a trading journal. There are, however, two things that you should always remember: You should update your journal regularly, and you should be honest with everything that you write in your journal.

Your journal should serve as a mirror of yourself. You are free to write everything that you want that is related to your life as an options trader. Ideally, your journal should include your reasons for trading options, your objectives, strategies that you are learning, your expected profit, mistakes and new learnings, and others.

In the first few weeks, you might not appreciate the value of having a journal, but you will soon start to appreciate its importance after some time. Just persist in writing your journal. When you start to see your progress, the more that you will appreciate having a trading journal.

If you are not fond of writing, you may want to use a file on your laptop or even an application on your mobile phone. The important thing is to have a journal where you can record and keep your thoughts and experiences. Also, be sure that your file is secure.

✓ Cash out

Another mistake that beginners often make is not making a withdrawal. Remember that you should cash out your profits from time to time. The reason why some traders only keep their profits in their account is so that they can grow their bankroll or the funds that they use for trading. Although this may seem like a practical reason, it is not a good practice. You should understand that the only way to fully realize your profits is to turn them into real cash, and the way to do that is by making a withdrawal. Do not worry; you can still grow the funds that you use for trading. You do not have to cash out all of your profits right away. If you want, you can just withdraw even just 40% of your profits, leaving the remaining 60% to grow your bankroll. Still, it is important to make a withdrawal every now and then. Cashing out is also an effective way to minimize your risk since the money that you cash out will no longer be lost in any trade. Come to think about it, if you do not make a withdrawal, then it will almost make no difference with managing a mere demo account.

✓ Avoid very quick trades

Avoid wagering on trades as fast as 1 minute or even less. Such timeline may be fun, but it does not reflect the true status of the market. Do not forget that the prices of the different assets continuously fluctuate. Especially if you are a beginner, it is advised to trade using at least the 5-minutes timeframe.

✓ Continuous research and analysis

Keep in mind that you are dealing with a continuously moving market. It is only right that you continue your research and analysis. The assets do not sleep just as the business that holds those assets continue to make progress and developments. Be up to date with the latest trends and analyze the different factors that can affect your investment. Part of this is to continually work on your strategy. Take note that options traders are active traders. You need to be on top of what you do. Since most trades involving options only last for a few minutes, you need to be constantly on the move making analyses and engaging in in-depth research. Take note that the more knowledge and understanding that you have, the greater your chances of making the right trading decision.

✓ Focus on the assets

Looking at the graphs and the charts can make the activity of trading options look sophisticated. Those small numbers on the screen, and those moving lines and stark colors, these are the things people want to see. They will make you think that you understand how to trade just by looking at these visual tools. However, you should understand that this is not enough. When you engage in options trading, you have to focus on the assets themselves and the businesses. Although you can still find patterns by relying on graphs, such is not enough. After all, these patterns do not always happen. And many times, the patterns are impossible to notice in the beginning. And even if you see them, there is no assurance that the trend will not change.

Focus on the assets. Research and study the assets that you are interested in. Read the news about them and look at the financial statements of their companies, as well as related businesses.

✓ Start small

If you are just starting out, it is strongly recommended that you start small. This means that you should keep your wagers low. When you are a beginner, your objective is not to make money right away. Instead, you should first familiarize yourself with the actual trading environment. In fact, it is advised that you should take advantage of a demo account first so that you will not be risking any real money. Once you have developed a good strategy, then you can easily add more funds and increase the amount that you trade with.

The term "small" is still a relative term. A good rule of thumb is to divide your funds by 100. This way you will have to commit 100 wrong decisions before your funds get exhausted.

✓ Diversify

In business, it is taught that you can effectively lower your losses by spreading your risk. The same principle applies when you engage in options trading. You should not wager all of your funds in a single trade. Instead of putting everything in a single trade, you can spread out your funds into multiple trades. Now, a common mistake is to become careless and take some of your trades for granted. Normally, this happens when you get lazy and stop doing enough research. You should always remember that it is better for you not to make a trade than to enter a trade without enough preparation.

✓ Use more than one strategy

It is strongly suggested that you apply at least two strategies. Every strategy will reveal something about a particular asset. As you already know, the more information that you have about an asset the more likely that you will be able to predict its price movement. The more strategies you are able to use, the better. However, you are not expected to use too many strategies as the price behavior of an asset can change quickly. By the time you finish your analysis, then the asset concerned might have already changed its behavior. So, stick to using just two or three strategies to back up your decisions. Experts strongly advise that you should always make use of fundamental analysis as it is the strategy that directly deals with the fundamentals. It is noteworthy that you have not applied fundamental analysis in just one day. Rather, you should follow on the news and be updated on the different assets on a daily basis.

✓ Money management

Even if you have an excellent strategy, you may end up with a negative profit if you do not know how to manage your funds properly. Be careful with how much you are risking and keep a close eye on your losses. You should focus on increasing your profits while minimizing your expenses. Remember not to spend the money that you cannot afford to lose. Also, when you manage your money, you should be as conservative with your expectations. Instead of expecting to double your funds in a day, aim to just profit even just by 10%. Be realistic.

✓ Take a break

The life of an options trader can be fun and exciting, but it is definitely not without any challenges. In fact, it can be tiring in the long run, especially if you properly do all the necessary research and preparation.

When you take a break, be sure to use it for relaxation. Do not use it to think about your trading strategies or anything that has to do with options trading. Remember that by giving your body enough time to rest and clearing your mind, you will be more able to think more effectively and come up with good trading decisions. Do not worry; you are expected to work more after the break. You have to learn how to making time for work as well as for rest. Options trading is a long journey. It simply does not end. So, be sure to take some rest every now and then. However, do not use this as an excuse for being lazy. Before you take a rest, you have to render some serious work first.

Chapter 5: Common Mistakes to Avoid

✗ Being an emotional trader

Although it is good to have a passion for what you do, it is not good if you allow your emotions to cloud your judgment. Never allow your emotions to direct your course of action. Instead, every trade has to be backed up by a solid research and analysis. A good way not to be too emotionally attached to your trades is by not spending the money that you cannot afford to lose. Therefore, do not use the money that you need to cover your household bills and other obligations. If you use the money that you cannot afford to lose, it is impossible not to be emotionally attached to your trades. When this happens, you will not be able to think clearly, and this is not good for you as an options trader. If, at any moment, you notice your emotions are influencing your mind, then stop and give your emotions just enough time to settle down. Once you can think more clearly, then that is the time when you can enter a trade, but never enter any trade if you are controlled by your emotions. Usually, people get controlled by their emotions after they experience a losing trade. The problem here is that your emotions might compel you to chase after your losses. You have to learn to control your emotions. Keep in mind that you are dealing with a market that does not care about you. In fact, it does not even know your name. Be objective and reasonable at all times just as the market is not driven by emotions.

×   Relying on expert advice

When you are a beginner, the tendency is to rely on the pieces of advice given by experts. You might rely on what websites and articles say about options trading. Although this may be good for beginners as far as becoming familiar with options trading is concerned, you should aim to develop your own understanding and view of options trading. It is also worth noting that many of these people who claim to be "experts" are not real experts. In fact, many of these so-called "experts" might even have more losses than profits. After all, these days, it is very easy to promote oneself as an expert with just a few clicks of a mouse, especially if you know how to take advantage of the power of social media. Also, even the real experts out there still commit mistakes from time to time, so always take whatever you read or learn with a grain of salt.

✗ Not developing your strategy

Do not forget that you are dealing with a continuously moving market. As such, you also have to keep on developing your strategy. Depending on what happens in the market, the prices of different assets can change their behavior.

Another common mistake is not testing your strategy. You should understand that a slight change in a strategy can have a strong impact on your overall strategy. This is why you always have to test your strategy several times even if you only make slight changes. This is a good time for you to take advantage of the demo account as provided by your broker.

✖ Being too aggressive

Avoid being too aggressive. There is no way to completely guarantee the success of a trade. Although it can be tempting to wager a very high amount to get a higher return, it is also a quick way to lose your money. Instead, focus on making small and consistent profits. You should put more emphasis on increasing your success rate. Especially if you are a beginner, it is not good to use any aggressive approach. Start out small and put all your focus on increasing your success rate.

✖ Short-term trades

It is common to see a trading period that lasts only for 30 seconds or a minute. Although this looks tempting, it is not advisable that you engage in such very short-term trades, unless if you are sure that the trading platform that you use is 100% trustworthy. The reason is that unscrupulous brokers take undue advantage of the short timeline. Usually, when you engage in a short trade, the value of the asset does not fluctuate that much. You may get the right option as much as the official record is concerned, but you would lose the wager. This is because there is a lapse of a few seconds for the platform to record the updated numbers, and these numbers are being continuously updated. This little delay can cost you your whole wager. Fortunately, not all platforms are like this. There are still reputable and reliable binary trading platforms out there. There are also strategies that are not meant for quick trades. For example, fundamental analysis is not a good strategy to use if you will just trade using a 1-minute timeline because it is not enough time to reflect the status of the market.

✕ Being a victim of the gambler's fallacy

The gambler's fallacy has caused many gamblers and investors to lose all their money. This is something that you should understand. So, what is the gambler's fallacy? It refers to the maturity of chances. The best way to explain it is by using an example. Let us say that in a coin flip, the head side came up four times in a row. What are the chances that the next coin flip will still be a head? Many people would think that the fifth coin flip will most probably be the tail side since head came up many times already. So, people will wager on the tail side. This is the gambler's fallacy. The truth is that even if the head side came up in four consecutive rows, the chances that the fifth coin flip will still be a head is still 50-50. Applying this in options trading, it means that even if *Call* comes five times in a row, it does not mean that the sixth trade that you will make will most likely be a *Put*. Now, you should also take into consideration that options trading is not supposed to be a gamble. The outcome of a trade does not come from a shuffled deck of cards or a random spin of a wheel. To increase your chances of making the right trading decision, you should do all the necessary research and apply your preferred strategy.

✗ Accepting the bonus

It is common for options trading brokers offer catchy bonuses in order to lure you to sign up and use their trading platform. A bonus may look as good as getting an additional 50% of your original deposit. Hence, if you deposit $100, you will have a total fund of $150 in your trading account. Although the bonus may look attractive, it does not come without a catch. The catch is that you will most probably be required to wager around forty times the bonus that you receive before you can make a withdrawal. The problem here is that before you meet the wagering requirement, you will most probably already lose your funds. The tendency is that in order to meet the wagering requirements, you will have to wager a much higher amount than usual. This will turn your strategy into an aggressive strategy, and your bankroll might not be ready for it. Of course, if you are able to devise a strategy that can satisfy the wagering requirement that normally comes with accepting the bonus, then you might want to take advantage of the bonus money.

×   Superstitious bets

There are some traders who make trades based on mere superstition. For example, a trader who wages all his funds in one trade on his birthday. Although there is nothing wrong with believing in superstition, you should not use it as a basis for making a trade. The market does not care about superstitions. Instead, you should study the asset that you want to trade. This way, you will have a better chance at making the right trading decision instead of merely relying on superstitions.

×   Trading as a hobby

There are many people who start trading options as a hobby. Although there is nothing wrong with this approach, it is not the recommended way to trade binary options. This is because trading as a mere hobby signifies lack of dedication, seriousness, and commitment. Instead of trading as a hobby, it is advised that you should approach trading as you would a business or any other profession. If you cannot give it enough time, then just be a part-time trader. This is better than not taking it seriously. You should understand that real and successful option traders take their work seriously. In fact, this is how they make continuous profits. They read numerous data and make solid research on a regular basis. They do not just consider it as a hobby, but they know just how important every trade is. Options trading is not supposed to be happy. If you want to achieve access, then it is time for you to be more serious about it by considering it to be some form of business or profession.

×   Not knowing when to stop

It is not uncommon to find traders who spend hours on their computer studying certain assets. Many times, they get too caught up in what they are doing that they do not notice the time. Just as you should know when to make a trade, you should also know when to call it a day and take some rest. Although generally, anyone above 18 years of age can start to trade options, this activity is not for everyone. If you notice that trading options continuously make you lose more money, then learn to stop, even just temporarily.

However, if you are quite stubborn to persist despite so many losses, then you might want to shift to making only small wagers until you develop a more effective strategy. Now, just as you should know when to stop when you encounter a series of losses, you should also know when to stop when you experience many successful trades.

It is not uncommon to find traders who enjoy significant profits, but only to encounter big and continuous losses after a while. This is another reason why you better withdraw your profits before you hit the ceiling.

✗ Compulsive trading

This is like emotional trading. However, in this case, you just want to feel that you are still in the game. This is where you make trades even if you do not see any good opportunities to make a profit. Remember to only make a wager if you are confident of your position. Do not take any trade for granted. Instead of submitting to this impulse, you should control yourself and focus on doing more research as you observe proper timing.

✗ Greed

Greed is something that you should definitely watch out for. Greed has led many traders to lose their money. It is hard to stop greed since you cannot see or touch it. It appears as a strong impulse inside you that compels you to desire more profits to the point that you can become careless. In order to avoid the consequences of being greedy, you should have a plan. It is good if you can come up with a short-term plan and a long-term plan. This way you will always have a good sense of direction no matter what happens to a trade. If, at any moment, you feel like you are being controlled by greed, then stop whatever it is that you are doing, do not make any trade, and just allow the strong impulse to settle down. After some time, you will be more able to think more clearly and take appropriate actions.

Chapter 6: The Successful Trader's Mindset

Your mindset is very important when you engage in options trading. Without the right mindset, you will most likely fail to make the right trading decisions. Let us examine how a successful trader thinks so that you will have an idea of how you should cultivate yourself as an options trader:

- Study and practice

Since you are dealing with a moving and living market, it is only right that you continue studying it. Many changes can happen in a day. There are also so many factors that affect the price movements of different assets. As an options trader, you should study the different theories and strategies and you should also continue practicing what you know. Do not forget that being a successful options trader is not all about theories—you also need to learn how to put your knowledge into actual practice. Study and practice should be a normal part of your daily routine as a trader.

- Self-discipline

As an options trader, everything depends on your decisions. Hence, you are also responsible for all of your actions. This is the kind of life where you are in control of everything. At the same time, you are responsible for everything. You have to exercise self-discipline. Every professional and successful trader knows that it takes hard and serious work to be a successful trader, especially if you want to remain successful for a long period of time. You have to stick to doing lots of research and render in-depth analysis of different underlying assets. In the beginning, it may be hard to impose discipline on yourself, but you have to realize how important being disciplined is. From time to time, you will have to force yourself to do research and analysis. You cannot afford to be lax and lazy. You cannot depend on anyone else for success but yourself. After some time, you will get used to the level of discipline that is required of professional traders. It is just really not that simple to change habits, but it is nonetheless doable.

- Calm

Successful traders are always calm. They are calm even when others are already panicking. They know that they should not allow themselves to be controlled by their emotions, and so they remain calm so that they could think more effectively. They do not panic even when they lose a trade because they have realized that losing some trades is a natural part of the game. After all, there is no amount of preparation that can guarantee a favorable outcome. However, this does not mean that you should no longer do your research. Remember that by doing research and analysis, you can significantly increase your chances of making the right trading decision and earning a nice profit. If you feel like you are losing your calm, then just relax and stop thinking about anything that has to do with options trading. Instead, just calm down and wait until you can think more objectively again. Sometimes all that you need to do is not to take any action and just wait.

- Open yet reasonable

Professional traders have an open mind. This is how they are able to come up with interesting ideas on how they can take advantage of certain assets. However, do not fall into the pitfall of being too open that you are led to believe something that is no longer possible. Remember to be open, but you should also stick to good reasons. Make sure that every trade that you make is backed up by solid research.

- Objective

Remain objective at all times. Do not forget that you are dealing with assets that do not feel any kind of emotion. You have to think rationally. Although it is good to sometimes daydream by focusing on the fruits of your actions, you should realize that it is more important to focus on the actions themselves. Do not be like the others who get too caught up in the outcome that they fail to take positive actions to actually make things happen.

- Patient

Successful traders are patient. Make sure to observe the proper timing. When it comes to timing, patience is important. Do not commit the common mistake of trading options during an unstable time or when it is hard to predict the price movements of assets. Learn to wait. Indeed, you will soon notice that there are times when you are able to speculate the price movements of different assets more easily, but there are also times when no matter what you do it would seem that you cannot predict how certain assets will behave. Be patient and make a trade only when you are confident of your decision.

- Not attached to their money

Professional and successful traders are not attached to the money that they can earn. Instead of being too busy thinking about how much you can earn, spend your time and efforts on learning the best strategy to use and how you can execute it more effectively. Realize that money will come on its own as long as you take the right actions.

- Persistent

Successful traders did not start out with a success story right away. In fact, most of them have encountered many losses before they truly learned to be an excellent trader. This is part of the journey to becoming a highly successful options trader. The important thing is for you not to give up. You should keep on trying despite many difficulties. The more that you take positive actions, the more you will learn and improve as a trader.

The mindset of a successful trader may not be easy to achieve right away. Again, persistence is the key. You need to give yourself time to adjust and adapt to a new way of thinking. After some time, you will get used to this kind of mindset that it will all be just second nature to you.

Conclusion

Thanks for making it through to the end of this book. We hope it was informative and able to provide you with all of the tools you need to achieve your goals whatever they may be.

The next step is to apply everything that you have learned and start raking in serious profits. Keep in mind that learning how to trade options effectively requires more than reading books. It is also a skill that needs to be developed. If you are just starting out, remember to start small or better yet, just stick first to using a demo account. Learning how to trade options effectively can create a strong positive impact on your life. However, options trading also has its own challenges and obstacles that you must overcome. By understanding and following the teachings in this book and practicing the strategies, you will be able to turn the options trading market into a goldmine of profits.

www.ingramcontent.com/pod-product-compliance
Lightning Source LLC
Chambersburg PA
CBHW071441210326
41597CB00020B/3896

* 9 7 8 1 9 2 2 3 2 0 2 0 9 *